Choose Your Own Adventure®!

"Your books are awesome! Keep writing!"
Jillian Miller, age 9

"I like this book because it's like you're
writing your own book!"
Kyle Smart, Age 5

"I think Choose Your Own Adventure books are thrilling.
I also like the way you change the way the story ends."
Molly Mobley, Age 9

"They have a mystery to them that makes it fun to read.
I like being able to solve them my own way. They have different
endings which make me want to read them more."
Gabe Pribil, Age 10

Illustrated by: Keith Newton
Book design: Jamie Proctor-Brassard of Letter10 Creative
For information regarding permission, write to:

CHOOSECO
P.O. Box 46
Waitsfield, Vermont 05673
www.cyoa.com

A DRAGONLARK BOOK

ISBN: 1-933390-61-1
EAN: 978-1-933390-61-1

Published simultaneously in the United States and Canada

Printed in Canada

0 9 8 7 6 5 4 3 2 1

CHOOSE YOUR OWN ADVENTURE®

DRAGON DAY

BY ANSON MONTGOMERY

ILLUSTRATED BY KEITH NEWTON

A DRAGONLARK BOOK

You are so excited. Today is Dragon
Day. Maybe *the best* Dragon Day!
You squirm out of bed. You hope, hope,
hope! this is the perfect day.

First on Dragon Day is the festival of games. Dragons come from all over the universe for outdoor games, plays, magic contests, flying races, and food. At the end of the day, dragonlarks who have done something great are called up to the stage in the Great Hall.

Every year, some young dragonlarks are picked to become grown-up dragons, and learn to fly. Of course, all your friends are still little dragonlarks. It's been a long time since you left the babies back in Egg Land, but you would like to learn to fly. Even your arch enemies, the Very Bad Dragons, are learning already. It has to be your turn soon.

Turn to the next page.

"Wyrm, Windy, Lala, wait up! It's me, Gander!" you shout when you see them standing in front of the doors of the Dragonlark Elementary gym.

"We know who you are, silly Gander," Lala says with a laugh, but she gives you a hug and you don't feel too bad. "We should go get tickets and decide what we want to do. I really want to see the show with the invisible giants. They throw paint at each other. It's messy."

Turn to page 4.

"Nah, giants are fun and all, but I want to see the flying races!" Wyrm says, jumping into the air and trying to fly. He wobbles in the air and then crashes down.

"My grandma is making the cake," Windy says, "ten dragons are flying it in from the goblin ovens. I'm not supposed to tell what it looks like. It's a surprise!"

"Can't we do both?" you ask. It would be fun to see the giants, but racing dragons are always exciting. Dragons are pretty competitive.

Turn to page 6.

"No, they are at the same time, Gander," Lala says, "there are lots of other things to do later; like eating Salamander Pies with Dream Cream topping!"

"Can I have a Salamander Pie now?" you ask, feeling a deep emptiness in your belly.

"NO!" Wyrm and Lala say together.

If you want to watch the Flying Dragon Races, turn to page 10.

If you choose to go to the Invisible Giant show, turn to page 15.

CLAMBER! TACKLE! CRASH! The two dragons tumble to the ground in a huge pile of twisting legs and wings.

You run forward and help the two dragons.

"Are you okay?" you ask the Red Team dragon.

"I'm okay, but I would have won if this Greenie hadn't crashed into me!"

"Sorry 'bout that," the Green Team dragon says from the ground.

"Oh, it's okay," says the Red Team dragon. "What a great race! Well, till the end!"

The End

You run as hard as you can. All four of your legs hit the ground, with your wings flapping.

"We're going to make it!" Lala gasps next to you.

"Almost there," Wyrm wheezes.

WHAM! You smash into the ankles of the tent-covered giants, and they tumble down together.

RIGHT INTO THE CAKE!

Cake goes flying everywhere. You are all tangled up with the giants, your friends, the flying dragons, the tent, and everything is covered in cake and frosting.

"Yum," you say, licking at a cake covered section of tent. "Lemon icing is my favorite!"

The End

"What am I going to do, guys?" you ask. "I don't have that much."

"Well, how much do you have, Gander?" Windy asks.

"Um, 17 Goblin Tails and 3 Goblin Nails," you answer, pulling the coins out to count.

"I'd cover for you buddy, but I don't have enough for both of us," Wyrm says.

"I don't have enough either, 50 Goblin Tails is a lot!" Lala says.

Turn to page 12.

Flying Dragon Races!
Just hearing the words bring up
memories of dragons soaring
through the air, each one straining
to win the race.

You think of how fun it must be to
be a racing dragon, with your tail flying
in the wind, wings flapping, going as
fast as you can to the flaming hoop
of victory.

"All right, lets get the tickets!" Lala shouts, "They're only 50 Goblin Tails each!" Your stomach jumps and squirms. And not in the good way. You don't have 50 Goblin Tails.

Turn to page 9.

"We should do the digging races instead!" Lala says, pretending to dig at the earth with her claws. "It's cool. And it is only 10 Goblin Tails. We'll have enough left over for pie!"

"Digging is NOT as cool as flying," Wyrm says.

Go on to the next page.

You have to agree, even though you like digging. Then you have a thought! You can't believe you didn't think of it earlier.

Your goblin bank! There must be 50 Goblin Tails in there. You'll have plenty of time to fill it back up before the spring trip! Or maybe not...

If you decide to open your goblin bank and go to the flying races, turn to page 33.

If you choose to go to the digging races instead, turn to page 50.

"Come on in, folks!" an old blue dragon yells at the door of the biggest tent you have ever seen. "Watch the amazing invisible giants! They're giant, and invisible!"

You give Wyrm your money, and he gets the tickets.

In the tent is a big ring, and you climb up into the stands to get a seat.

In the back of the tent, you see a snaky black tail sneaking around. You look at it. You've seen that tail before, but where?

Turn to the next page.

"Lady and Gentle-Dragons, welcome to the invisible giant show!" the announcer says, sweeping his foreleg towards the ring.

There is nothing there except ten big cans of paint.

Then one of the cans rises from the floor as if on a string, and paint goes flying out of it!

Now you see a HUGE paint covered hand grab a bucket of yellow paint and throw it across the ring.

The can of paint hits another giant in the face!

"YOWWWWWW!" it yells. "FACE HURT!"

Turn to page 18.

The yellow-paint invisible giant keeps yelling, and you put your paws up to your ears. A hurt giant makes a lot of noise!

"Something's wrong!" Windy says, pointing to the center of the ring. Paint is flying everywhere, and it hits the shapes of giant arms and giant legs, scrambling around in the confusion. But Windy isn't pointing to that.

The pole holding the tent up bends and moves, and tiny splinters crack off. It's breaking!

"Watch out everyone!" Windy yells as it snaps and falls.

Turn to page 21.

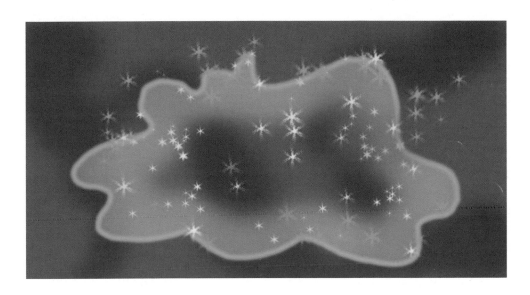

"Space boogers sound like they hurt," Windy says wonderingly.

"This is no time to talk about Space boogers!" the head judge says seriously, shaking his head.

"Certainly not!" says another judge, joining in. "Who ever heard of such a thing! How would they form?" She makes a face at you. "Silly little Dragonlark!"

Turn to page 26.

The pole snaps in half and falls straight for the stands. Everyone scrambles out of the way.

The tent fabric lands on top of the paint-covered invisible giants and they are covered up. Giants yell and try to rip free. The collapsed tent starts running away! Someone might get hurt.

"Help, my dragon baby is missing!" purple dragon mom shouts. She needs help.

"Someone has to stop those giants!" Wyrm says, "They'll stomp someone flat without knowing it!"

"We need to help find the dragon baby!" Lala says, pulling at your paw.

If you help look for the dragon baby, turn to page 59.

If you try and stop the tent-covered, runaway invisible giants, turn to page 64.

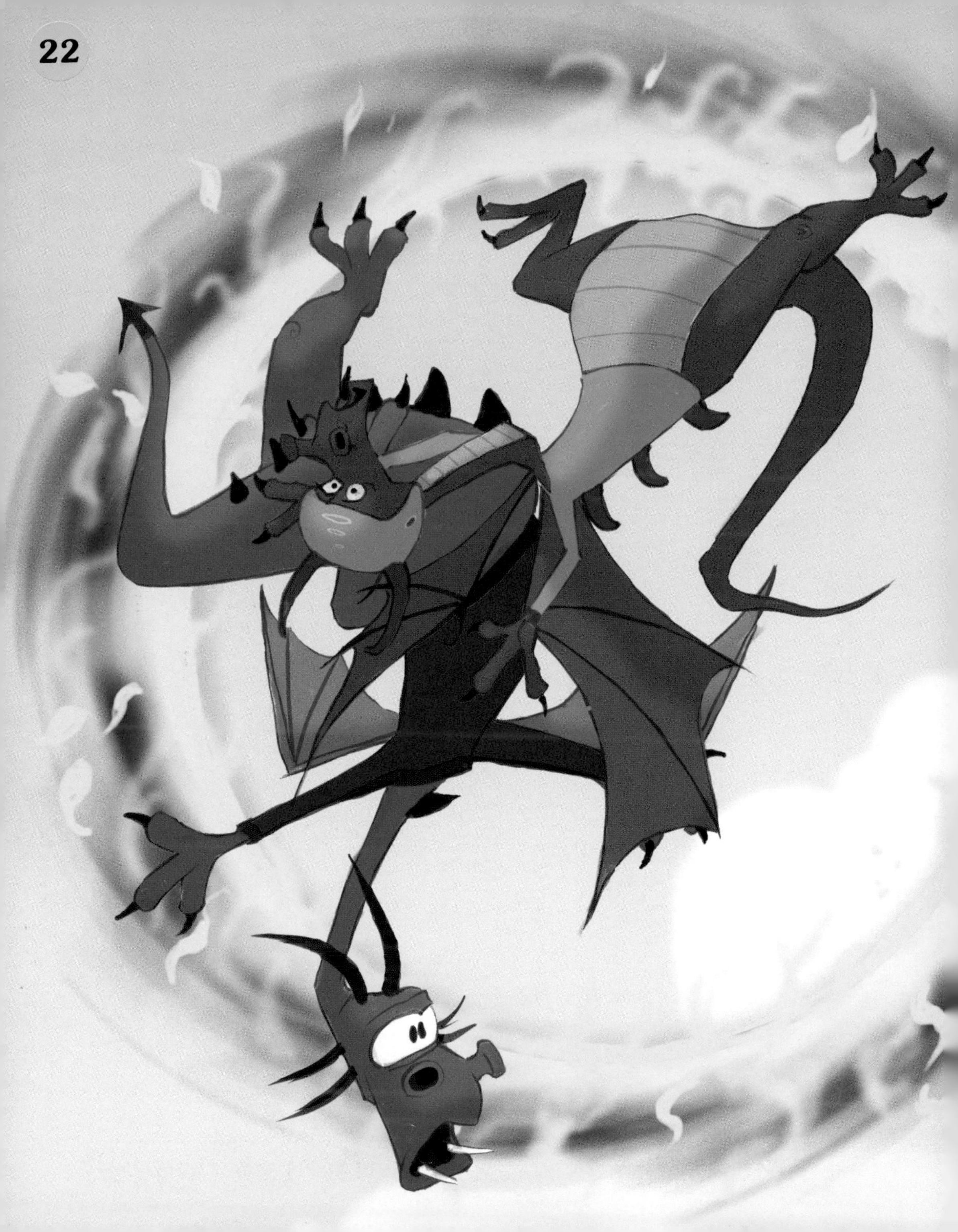

"Go Green!" you shout, joining in the fun.

The dragons race through the air, flying so fast that you can't believe your eyes. You don't think you'll ever be so fast, even when you are grown-up.

The Red Team seems to be winning!

"They're going to win!" Lala yells.

Just as the Red Team dragon is about to go through the flaming hoop at the end, the Green Team dragon catches up with one last burst of speed. Instead of going through the hoop, the Green dragon smacks into the Red dragon. Both crash to the ground!

Turn to page 7.

You run up to the digging race judges and freeze!

What do you do?

"Za Za Za Blue Moon Space Boogers!" you yell, not knowing what else to say.

Everyone turns to stare at you.

Lala smiles and gives you two thumbs up.

Turn to page 19.

"I'm feeling a little better," Cupcake says. "Actually, I'm feeling a LOT better. I want to DIG!"

"I wouldn't get in her way," Lala says to the main judge. She looks at Cupcake and nods her head.

"Go, Cupcake, Go Tulip!" you shout as the dirt goes flying all around you. It is a huge mess. And lots of fun!

Everyone is laughing.

Tulip's team comes in second place, but only by a little bit.

"You're a hoot, Gander," Tulip tells you. "I think a Dragon like you is great to have around!"

The End

"Come on, get your cow-on-a-stick!" a tiny man yells. He holds a tray of candy cow-on-a-sticks. You only see these once a year! Your stomach growls.

"Let's get some," Lala says.

Turn to page 30.

You each get a cow-on-a-stick candy and look around you. In a corner, a huge dragon sits at a picnic table, eating his fourth cow-on-a-stick. You can tell because there are three other sticks on the picnic table he is sitting at.

"Are you Pilly?" you ask, walking up to the dragon. He is bigger than both of your parents put together. And they aren't small!

"Yup," he says in a deep voice.

Turn to page 32.

"Your mom is looking for you!" Lala says, then adds. "She said you were a baby."

"Yeah," Pilly says. "She does that. I guess I'll always be her little dragon baby!"

Wyrm makes gagging noises and you laugh.

"Want a bite?" Pilly asks, handing you the cow-on-a-stick.

"You bet," you say.

The End

"Run, Gander, run! Break that goblin bank! We don't want to miss the first race!" Wyrm says.

You run home so fast! You are out of breath when you get there.

"Whew. Whooooo-whew," you gasp, throwing the goblin bank on the floor. It breaks open with a loud smash.

Turn to page 35.

You count the money on the floor.

It isn't enough. You only have 43 Goblin Tails!

But wait–what's that orange thing sticking out from under your backpack? You dive across the floor and pick it up. One more Goblin Tail! Maybe you have more you've forgotten about. You rip apart your room. No more money appears. Just carpet fuzz and a chew toy for your pet basilisk. That isn't going to get you into the races!

What are you going to do?

You have an idea. Your grandma is home!

Turn to the next page.

Grandma Coalsmasher gives you the 6 Goblin Tails. She is the best!

"Good luck, Gander!" says Grandma.

"Love you, Grandma!" you say, running to the races.

You rush to the ticket counter and hand over your 50 Goblin Tails. An older air dragon hands you back a colorful token.

"The race starts in two minutes!" she tells you. "Go over to the wading pool, that's where you can place your bet."

Since the only things you can win are cookies, pies, cakes and pastries, you hope that it is a cake! Sweet, sweet, cake.

Turn to page 39.

You reach the lookout hill, where everyone's tokens rest on lily pads.

"Different lily pads for different teams," a nice older dragon explains to you. "Then when the race is over, winners pick a prize."

The dragons take off from the starting gate and you can't breathe until they stop.

Swirling in the air, they vie for the lead. Red and Green, racing for the win!

"Choose a team! Cake for the winners! Pie for the losers!" someone yells.

"Or the other way around!" yells someone else.

Turn to the next page.

"The Greens are the coolest," Wyrm announces, "Definitely the coolest!"

"Yeah, if you like slow flyers," Lala responds. "The Reds will fly rings around the Greens."

The dragons line up in the flying starting gate. Steam blows from the dragons' noses.

You have to choose! Which team will you support?

If you choose the Green Team, turn to page 23.

If you choose the Red Team, turn to page 57.

"Come on Gander, you can do-ooooo-IT!" Windy screams in your face.

"Uhh, Windy, he's just putting his uniform on," Lala says helpfully. "No need to spray it, and that's coming from a water Dragonlark!"

"Yeah, spray it Windy!" Wyrm says, joining in.

"Calm down, Wyrm," Windy says, looking embarrassed.

You don't know what to say. You are scared about the digging race. You wish you had gone to the flying races instead. 50 Goblin Tails or not.

Turn to page 44.

"Time to start the race!" yells the head referee.

Turn to page 46.

Windy finds you after the second race. This one was pretty exciting!

The dragons were both chained to huge rocks and they had to use the rocks to smash a dangling troll made of hay. While blindfolded. At the same time.

"Did you see how close that boulder came to the green dragon?" Lala asks. "I thought he was going to get smacked!"

"I think it's a bit silly," Windy sniffs, then adds "but fun!"

A large dragon so covered in dirt that you don't recognize it comes up to you and your friends. It is wearing some sort of team uniform, but you can't tell for what.

Turn to page 52.

You are in front of a huge mountain of dirt. On top of the dirt are giant rocks. You have to move the whole mountain to the other side of the field. It is a BIG mountain. You feel small.

"Come on Gander! Let's get busy," Tulip says, knocking you on the shoulder. You almost fall over but smile at her anyway.

Then you move rocks and dirt. And more rocks and dirt. You don't know how much more you can do! "Come on Gander, move those rocks!" your friends yell, and you keep moving them, no matter how heavy they feel.

When the last speck of dirt has been moved into the circle, you collapse.

"Wake up, Gander!" yells Lala. "You're in third place!"

Turn to page 48.

When you wake up you are in the Dragon Day Hall! How did you get here?

"...and special thanks to Gander, for helping the Steam Shovel Shovelers! In recognition of his efforts to help someone who needed a hand, we would like to offer him a special shout out on this Dragon Day! Yay Gander!"

You get up and raise your paws. The dragons cheer.

"Thank you!" you say. What a great Dragon Day!

The End

"Wow, look at that dirt fly," Lala says.

"No kidding," Wyrm agrees, impressed. "It's like a river of mud coming from those dudes!"

You look at the huge earth dragons clawing their way through a hill. With each scoop of their powerful paws, they move tons of earth. The air is steamy and smells of dirt.

Turn to page 45.

"Hey guys, do you have any Dragon Salts?" the dirt-covered dragon asks.

"Why?" Windy asks. "Who are you?"

"My name is Tulip. Do you have them or not?" she says, looking a bit angry, even under the dirt. "My friend is sick."

"Oh, of course," Windy says, embarrassed. "I have them right here!"

Turn to page 55.

"Hang in there, Cupcake," Tulip says to a massive dragon wearing the same uniform she wears.

Cupcake splutters when Windy holds the Dragon Salts under her nose. Then she sneezes a huge blast of green flames. Wyrm jumps out of the way at the last second.

"When's the race?" Cupcake asks weakly, wiping bits of green flame off her lips with her left paw.

"Doesn't matter," Tulip says. "We'll have to forfeit. There's no way you can dig right now."

Turn to page 56.

"Wait! I have an idea!" Lala says, hopping up and down. "Why don't we go and distract the judges so they can't start on time and Cupcake can rest!"

"I'm sure they won't fall for a trick like that, Lala," Windy says. "Besides, I think Cupcake probably should rest.

If you listen to Lala and distract the judges so Cupcake can rest, turn to page 24.

If you decide to take Cupcake's place on the digging team, turn to page 42.

"Green's are mean! Red is Fred!" Wyrm shouts as the dragons race furiously through the air.

"What does 'Fred' mean, Wyrm?" Windy asks.

"I don't know," Wyrm answers with a laugh. "But it rhymes!"

Lala makes a circle with one claw by her head. You laugh.

The Red Team dragon makes one last sweep of its wings and flies through the flaming hoop! The Red Team won!

Turn to the next page.

"Time to go to the Dragon Day Ceremony!" Lala says with a bite of cake AND pie in her mouth.

"Yuck!" Windy says to Lala. "Just swallow, please, for me?"

Lala just opens her mouth wider.

"Let's go," you say, walking towards the Great Hall.

Turn to page 60.

"I say we go to the cow-on-a-stick place," Wyrm says. "So, if he isn't there, we can still get a cow-on-a-stick!"

"Wyrm!" Lala says. "I think we should go to the Great Hall, that is where they bring the lost children."

"Yeah, water-brains," Wyrm shoots back, "but that is only AFTER they find them!"

"Listen, smoke-breath," Lala says, getting mad. "Maybe someone else has found Pilly and brought him there. We should a least check."

If you want to go to the cow-on-a-stick shop to look for Pilly, turn to page 28.

If you decide to look for him in the Great Hall, turn to page 69.

"After those giants!" Wyrm yells, rushing after the tent-covered giants.

Dragons scatter in front of the moving fabric. You see a little, snaky black tail again, just like you noticed before right before the pole broke.

"Very Bad Dragons!" you whisper. "They're the ones making this happen!"

"Oh no!" says Lala. She is always scared when the Very Bad Dragons are around.

"What do the Very Bad Dragons want?" asks Windy.

"They want that cake!" says Wyrm, pointing.

Turn to page 66.

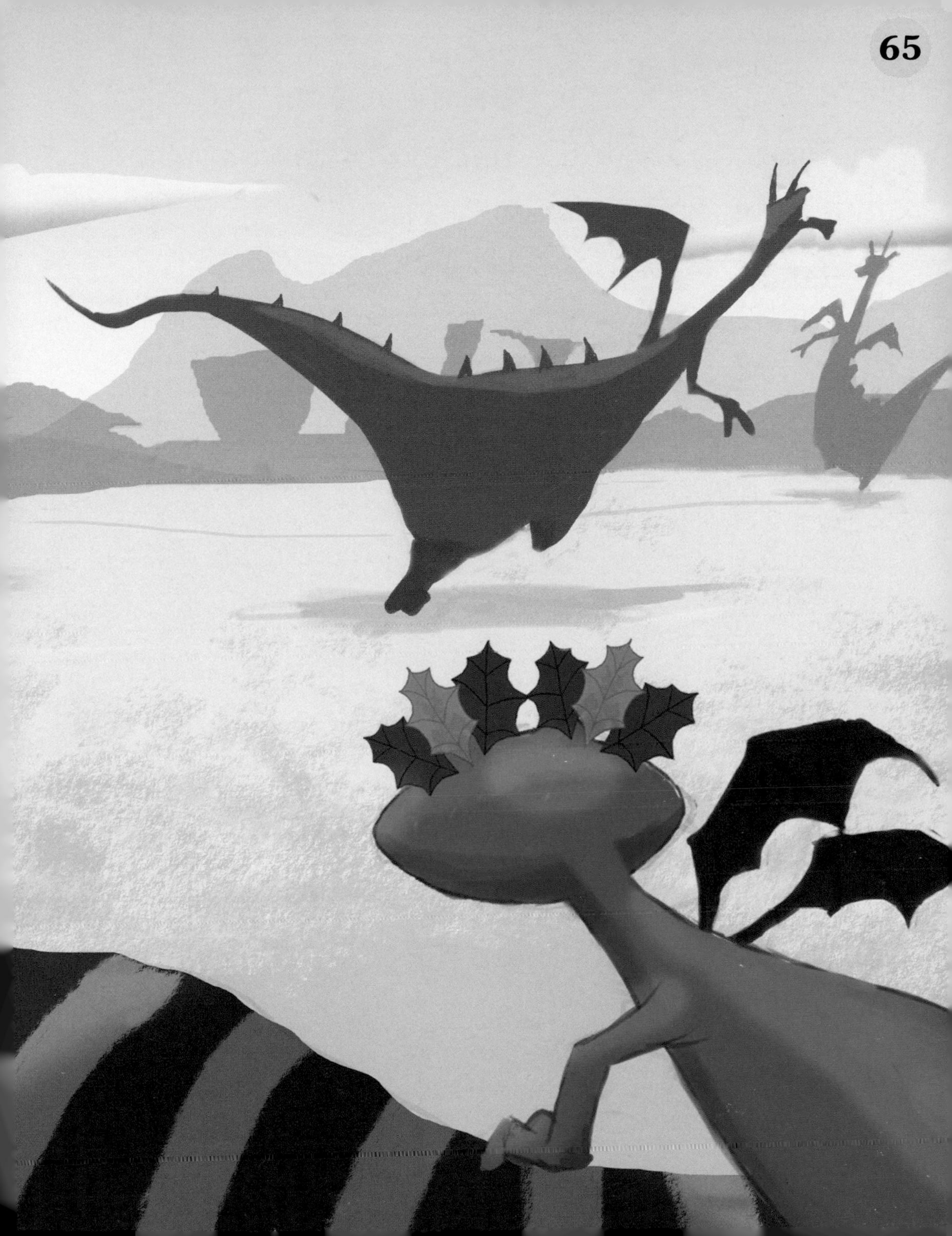

Flying in from the far side of the games are ten dragons. They are holding an enormous cake shaped like a ship with a water dragon guarding it.

Running right at them are the tent-covered giants. None of the flying dragons seems to notice the crash they are about to have.

"Oh, no!" you say. "They'll smash the cake!"

"We have to stop them!" Lala says.

"Or warn the cake dragons!" Wyrm adds.

Turn to page 68.

Windy is across the field, close to the cake her grandmother made. She is watching the flying dragons cross toward the Great Hall.

"If we run right now, we can tackle the giants before they ruin the Dragon Day Cake!" Wyrm says.

"But Windy is over there!" you say, pointing. "If we warn her, they can fly away and save the cake. It sure looks yummy." Your stomach growls. You have to save this cake!

If you try and tackle the giants, turn to page 8.

If you try and warn Windy, turn to page 71.

The Great Hall is almost empty when you get there. You know it will be full when they get to the Dragon Day ceremony.

"Excuse me," Lala asks a nice-looking silver dragon at the information desk, "we're looking for a lost dragon baby named

Pilly. Have you seen him?"

"Sorry, honey," she says shaking her head.

"No one's brought him in. But I'll keep an eye out."

Turn to the next page.

"We'll just have to keep looking," Wyrm says encouragingly, but he looks worried. You have been searching for an hour and Dragon Day is almost done.

You are about to give up when you notice something moving around beneath the tent the giants had run away with. It is in a messy pile by the edge of the huge games field.

"Help! I'm stuck!" you hear a faint voice yelling from the pile.

"Hang on Pilly! We'll get you out!" Lala says comfortingly.

It takes a while, but you finally get Pilly out of the tent.

"Mom, stop kissing me. I'm okay!" he says when you bring him back to his mom.

"You are all heroes!"

The End

"Windy! Watch out! Giants! Tents! Cake!"

You, Lala, and Wyrm yell and scream as you run across the field.

The giants are about to smash into the cake, when Windy finally notices you.

She looks behind her and sees the tent about to smash into the cake, and she waves her baton higher.

Turn to page 73.

"Fly up! Now!" Windy yells, waving her baton.

The dragons all fly higher, lifting the ship cake up into the sky.

The giants collapse into a huge pile.

"Whew, that was close!" Lala says, sitting down.

"Too close!" Wyrm agrees. Later, when everyone is in the Great Hall for the Dragon Day Ceremony, they bring you and your three friends up onto the stage.

"In honor of your saving the cake today, we would like to give you each a slice of cake first!"

"Just one?" you ask, worried. The slices look pretty small.

"Gander!" Windy says.

"We'll make sure yours is a big one," the dragon cutting the cake tells you with a laugh.

The End

ABOUT THE ILLUSTRATOR

Illustrator Keith Newton began his art career in the theater as a set painter. Having talent and a strong desire to paint portraits, he moved to New York and studied fine art at the Art Students League. Keith has won numerous awards in art such as The Grumbacher Gold Medallion and Salmagundi Award for Pastel. He soon began illustrating and was hired by Walt Disney Feature Animation where he worked on such films as Pocahontas and Mulan as a background artist. Keith also designed color models for sculptures at Disney's Animal Kingdom and has animated commercials for Euro Disney. Today, Keith Newton freelances from his home and teaches entertainment illustration at the College for Creative Studies in Detroit. He is married and has two daughters.

ABOUT THE AUTHOR

After graduating from Williams College with a degree specialization in ancient history, **Anson Montgomery** spent ten years founding and working in technology-related companies, as well as working as a freelance journalist for financial and local publications. He is the author of four books in the original Choose Your Own Adventure series, *Everest Adventure, Snowboard Racer, Moon Quest* (reissued in 2008 by Chooseco), and *CyberHacker* as well as two volumes of *Choose Your Own Adventure® The Golden Path™*, part of a three volume series. Anson lives in Warren, VT with his wife, Rebecca, and his two daughters, Avery and Lila.